THE COMPLETE BOOK OF

169 *Redouté* Roses

THE COMPLETE BOOK OF

169 Redouté Roses

BY FRANK J. ANDERSON

HONORARY CURATOR OF RARE BOOKS

NEW YORK BOTANICAL GARDEN

ABBEVILLE PRESS • PUBLISHERS • NEW YORK

FRONT COVER
Bramble Rose
Rosa multiflora carnea
Commentary on page 96

TITLE PAGE
Royal French Rose
Rosa gallica regalis
Commentary on page 16

The illustrations in this book are from the collection of the New York Botanical Garden and are reproduced by permission of the Garden's president, Dr. Howard S. Irwin, and the director of the Library, Mr. Charles R. Long.

Library of Congress Cataloging in Publication Data

Redouté, Pierre Joseph, 1759–1840.
   The complete book of 169 Redouté roses.

   1. Roses—Pictorial works.   2. Roses in art.
3. Redouté, Pierre Joseph, 1759–1840.
I. Anderson, Frank J., 1912–   II. Title.
SB411.R413   635.9′33′216   79–4247
ISBN 0-89659-039-9

CONTENTS

INTRODUCTION

REDOUTÉ'S *Les Roses* is one of those acknowledged masterpieces such as Vesalius's *The Fabric of the Human Body*, in which the paths of science and art intersect with glorious and immortal results. It also refutes all those misguided connoisseurs who have pitched opposite camps for or against realism in art. The accurate reflection of the visible does not in itself necessarily infer the presence of the highest form of art; many an academic painting or sculpture of the nineteenth century will amply demonstrate the contrary. Conversely, the total abandonment of design, form, and meaning in modern works does not guarantee that they are voicing profound and eternal truths. Art must transcend both appearance and the styles of its age when it shapes its statements, whether they be abstractions or mirrors of nature, and Redouté's roses do exactly that. We respond instinctively to the rightness of them, for they represent the present state of dynamic, organic forms achieved through eons of evolutionary progress. They are not simply the truth for now; rather, they open our imagination to the multileveled realities of the future.

Although Pierre-Joseph Redouté (1759–1841) was the major creator of *Les Roses*, he was by no means its sole author. The spirit and material contributions of many others were also involved—chiefly Claude Antoine Thory, who supplied the descriptive text, and the Empress Josephine. Her love of flowers and her gardens at Malmaison furnished the inspiration that brought *Les Roses* into being. Josephine's generous patronage of Redouté, and of those botanists and gardeners she had gathered for the purpose of creating the most beautiful rose garden the world had ever known, made *Les Roses* an inevitable production. Although she did not live to see the work published (she died in

1814, three years before publication began), the people involved, as well as the flowers themselves, had long formed an intimate part of her everyday life.

Situated about seven and a half miles west of Paris, just outside the country town of Rueil, La Malmaison was less than ten miles from many of the historic gardens of France, including Marly, Versailles, and Redouté's own gardens at Fleury-sous-Meudon. After Josephine's death, the estate was preserved intact as the property of her son Eugéne, but it later passed through many owners, among them Charles X and Napoleon III. The gardens, of course, fell into neglect without Josephine's guiding hand, and finally met with complete destruction during the Prussian invasion of 1870. In 1904, however, a philanthropic Frenchman named Osiris bought the house together with the grounds, which were much reduced by then, and gave it to the government as a museum. It has since been refurnished as Josephine knew it, and the gardens are now undergoing restoration.

By the time Redouté came to Malmaison to paint its roses, he had already served as draftsman in the Queen's Cabinet of Marie Antoinette. He was also official flower painter of the Muséum d'Histoire Naturelle, and this position probably helped him survive the French Revolution. He was later designated flower painter to Empress Josephine, and held the same position in the time of Louis Philippe.

Throughout that turbulent period, Redouté instructed the aristocracy and the wealthy in the art of painting flowers, becoming highly popular and prosperous in the process. Josephine gave him an annual salary of eighteen thousand francs—more than twenty-five thousand 1979 dollars. She must also have infected him with her own extravagant habits, for he was in deep financial straits at the time of his death. The career he had begun at age thirteen, when he left his father's studio to practice his art, ended at eighty-two in Paris, as a student placed a flower in his hand for him to study. Along the way, fame, riches, and hardship had all been his lot; and the world was incalculably richer for his work. He had supplied about five thousand illustrations for some twenty-eight botanical works, including the incomparable *Les Roses,* and an equal number of paintings for the *Cabinet des Velins,* the official collection of France's national museum of natural history. Above all, he left a legacy of beauty for all who came after him to enjoy.

The third major contributor to *Les Roses* was Claude Antoine Thory (1759–1827). A graduate of the College of Lisieux and a barrister by profession, he eventually became a registrar at the Châtelet in Paris, one of the most powerful law courts in Revolutionary France. He was among those who signed the decree of arrest that jailed Marat from October to December of 1789. Later, as the Revolution went its unpredictable way, and especially after the assassination of Marat, Thory himself was persecuted by the revolutionists.

When the courts at the Châtelet were suppressed in August of 1790, Thory retired to his gardens at Belleville and devoted his time to study and writing. In earlier times, he had made collections of minerals, shells, insects, and plants; now he turned his attention chiefly to botany, particularly to roses. For many years he conducted research, using governmental files on botany, and spoke with professional and amateur gardeners, as well as with scientists, on his chosen topic. Out of that labor came a systematization of the genus *Rosa,* in which Thory attempted to sort out the tangled relationships of species, varieties, hybrids, and all else connected with the history of cultivated roses.

Redouté chose Thory to write the text for *Les Roses* because of his wide knowledge of that genus, but to save time, since subscribers were anxiously awaiting issuance of each of the thirty parts promised them, Redouté gave him pictures to work with in the haphazard order of their completion. Thus there is a total lack of botanical system in the first edition. When

time permitted, Thory set forth his arrangement of the genus *Rosa* in the second edition; and he continued his friendship and correspondence with Redouté until Thory died in 1827. The wit and elegance of Thory's style brought his work into great repute, which was further heightened by the care and accuracy of his research. This meticulousness has helped his work to retain its value to the present day.

The rose, that plant that bound together Thory, Redouté, and Josephine in common endeavor, has long exerted its attraction upon humanity. No one can say when it first made its bow among the flowering plants, but it is estimated to be between 35 million and 70 million years of age. Almost certainly native to northern temperate regions, it was a simple five-petaled flower at the outset. Gradually some of its stamens modified into extra petals (actually staminodes), and the flower gained the multipetaled or double form best exemplified by the cabbage, or centifolia, rose.

Its scent and color soon brought the rose into notice, and its hue seems to be the cause of its name, for in whatever language it is spoken of the words for the flower and its color are synonymous. It found its way into medicine, as into perfumery, through its fragrance, since aromatic things were believed to drive away disease. The rose's ornamental value in gardens was obvious, and it was also prized for decorative effects at banquets and within the house. Egypt, under Roman rule, exported shiploads of roses to Rome, where they were used for such extravagant purposes as showering diners at Nero's feasts until they were almost calf-deep in petals.

The growing of roses has always been surrounded by a mystique, which has sometimes frightened off prospective rose gardeners—unnecessarily so. One has only to remember that many roses grow in the wild with no care at all, but flourish nonetheless in many kinds of climates and soils. Given half a chance in a garden situation, almost any healthy rose bush will not only survive but will blossom abundantly year after year.

To make sure you start with healthy plants, purchase your shrubs only from reputable nurseries in your own area. While roses may be shipped by mail or express, it is usually advisable to buy them locally if possible. As a rule, you should choose dormant two-year-old plants with roots that have been protected against drying out. They should be field-grown, and their tags should so state, together with other pertinent facts. If by any chance they become dried out before you can plant them, bury them in damp soil for a day or two and they will revive.

Before starting to plant, choose a site that meets the specific demands of the species or variety you have. Suggestions are often found on the supplying nursery's label. Some roses require shade or semishade, but most thrive in sunshine, generally requiring a minimum of six hours of sunlight. Be sure to place the rose in adequately drained ground, neither too moist nor too dry. The planting area should be free of tree roots, weed infestation, and any other competitors that would drain away nourishment from the rose itself.

Begin planting by digging an ample hole, large enough to accommodate the full spread and depth of the shrub's roots without any crowding. Thoroughly break up the soil removed, leaving no clods or lumps, and then mix in the equivalent of one quarter of its volume in organic material, such as rotted manure, compost, humus, or peat.

Line the bottom of the hole with several inches of drainage material, such as cut stone or broken crockery. Then insert the shrub, spreading its roots both downward and outward, and give it support while you refill the hole. Replace the soil gradually, spading the loose earth in and firming it gently as you do. From time to time pour in a bucketful of water to eliminate any air pockets.

Most roses are sold grafted onto understock and have a noticeable bump at the site of the graft union, between the roots and the stem. If you are planting in sandy, loamy soil, place that bump below the ground line; but if the earth is stiff and heavy, place it above soil level. Gently tamp all soil into place when the earth has been replaced. To finish, sprinkle half a handful of 5–10–5 fertilizer formula atop the soil around the bush. Never put the fertilizer *in* the hole, because it will burn the roots.

Full and frequent watering is appreciated by all roses, and they should be given an occasional deep and heavy soaking. Since climates and soils vary widely, it is best to consult your local garden center about proper fertilization.

Pruning is best done before new growth begins in spring. Remove all dead, old, diseased, and damaged wood, and if necessary trim away any winter injury. Cut away only as much of the healthy stock as is necessary to properly shape the shrub. When trimming stems, remember that it takes about six leaves to produce and feed each flower, so snip with discretion. If the pith of the stems looks brown, cut down until a creamy pith can be seen. Always cut *above* a bud, and if the stem is more than a quarter of an inch thick, protect the wound with a dressing of caulking compound or any similar, turpentine-free substance.

While the physical labor involved in digging, pruning, and spraying may prove bothersome at times, it brings with it the reward that kings and commoners alike have enjoyed for centuries. That reward, of course, is the pleasure of being in a rose-colored world—of one's own creation.

F . J . A .

9

THE COMPLETE BOOK OF

169 Redouté Roses

Blood Rose of China

[ROSA CHINENSIS CRUENTA]

THE BLOOD ROSE OF CHINA bloomed in Europe for the first time in the English nurseries of the Messrs. Colville in 1800. Once thought to have originated in India, it is now known to be native to China, and this variety, with its recurrent blossoms, was probably an offspring of *Rosa chinensis semperflorens*.

At first *R. chinensis cruenta* flowered in hot-beds or orangeries, but in time it was grafted onto the roots of the dog rose, a very common nineteenth-century practice, or onto those of the ordinary Chinese rose. As a variety it soon came to be considered the most beautiful and most double of all the red roses. The shrub rises about two feet high and has very large flowers, borne in clusters of three after maturity. When still young, however, the flowers are produced singly. The name blood rose comes, of course, from the color of its petals, and is included in the scientific term for this variety, which is Latin for "bloody."

Burgundy Rose

[ROSA CENTIFOLIA PARVIFOLIA]

WITH A HEIGHT OF about eighteen inches and flowers no more than roughly an inch across, this lovely rose easily qualifies as a miniature. It is nonetheless a true member of the cabbage rose group, and was first discovered as early as 1664 in the French province of Burgundy. Because its small, tightly closed blossoms resemble the ornamental topknots on the hats of French sailors, *Rosa centifolia parvifolia* was once called the pompon rose, *R. pomponia*. It was also known as *R. burgundiaca,* the Burgundy rose, from its place of origin.

Whether or not this rose is a mutation of the cabbage rose or a hybrid derived from *R. gallica* remains a question. It has a sweet scent, a remarkably pretty rose color, and attractive foliage of a clear green hue; these qualities combined with its diminutive size guarantee it long-lasting favor with gardeners.

Royal French Rose

[ROSA GALLICA REGALIS]

THE GARDENERS OF nineteenth-century France knew this variety as the great rose of St. Francis, but today we call it the royal French rose. Its blossoms, three or more inches across, are of a very double form, beautifully two-toned pink in color but with very little scent. All its energies seem to have been thrown into producing its magnificent flower heads.

The royal French rose is usually grafted onto other root stocks, for on its own roots it becomes bushy and often fails to reach more than two and a half feet in height. In England a subvariety called the cabbage Province (which should really be Provins) has been developed. It bears abundant blossoms of a very agreeable odor, and the nineteenth-century English distillers preferred it to all other species in making their perfumes.

Rosa gallica regalis has one defect, which is easily corrected. If grown under the strong, unshaded summer sun, it often becomes covered with a white, powdery dust, rather like mildew, all over the plant. If it is given semishade, however, that difficulty need never arise.

Large-flowered Dog Rose

[ROSA CANINA GRANDIFLORA]

As FAR BACK AS ancient Greek times, the flowers that we now call dog roses were associated with canines. They were then known under the name of Cynosbatos, which means dog-berry, and the berrylike rose hips were used to prepare a medicinal syrup used to cure infected dog-bites.

This variety was considered to have the largest flowers of any in the dog rose group, and was particularly noted for its burst of bloom. The sudden display was often likened to a lightning flash, leading one horticulturist to name it *Rosa canina fulgens* (the ''bright'' or ''flashing'' dog rose). Thory, however, renamed it for a more consistent characteristic, the size of its petals, since those who viewed the plant after the initial blooming effect was over would not understand the cause behind the descriptive *fulgens*.

Most dog rose seeds take about two years to germinate, but they eventually reward the grower's patience with their long-lived roots, which are often used as an understock for grafts. *R. canina grandiflora* produces an abundance of seeds that mature even in the absence of fertilization. This process, called apomixis, is a distinguishing characteristic of the dog roses.

Kamchatka Rose

[ROSA RUGOSA KAMTCHATICA]

ALL THE RUGOSA ROSES are hardy, especially this variety, as might be expected from its point of origin—northeast Siberia on the peninsula of Kamchatka. Once thought to be a distinct species, it is now known as another of the many varieties of *Rosa rugosa,* and is thought to be a natural hybrid of *R. rugosa* crossed with a closely allied species, *R. davurica.*

The mauve-pink flowers of *R. rugosa kamtchatica* are usually borne in solitary fashion at the tops of its exceptionally thorny stems, but sometimes they also grow in pairs. The highly aromatic blossoms flower in June and tend, in milder climates, to bloom again in autumn. In medieval Japan they were combined with camphor and musk to make a highly popular perfume.

The Kamchatka variety is horticulturally superior to the original *R. rugosa* and is susceptible to only one serious but rare pest, the rose stem girdler. Otherwise it is most resistant to the general run of rose diseases and can thrive in dry soil, high winds, and even the salt air of the seashore. Its major fault is that the flowers do not last when cut; but few would be tempted to cut them anyway after seeing their horrendous armament of thorns.

Pompon Rose

[ROSA CENTIFOLIA POMPONIA]

THE BLOSSOMS OF THE POMPON ROSE are only about one inch wide, but they make up for their diminutive size with their sweet fragrance. The petals are of a lively pink color, which gradually darkens toward the center of the flower. Like most centifolias, this rose seldom pollinates naturally because its petals are packed so densely together.

The pompon rose has some peculiarities worth mentioning. Its stems form a bushy growth leading out from the main branches, a rarity in itself. What is even stranger is that almost every year, immediately after flowering, both the stems and branches begin to dry and fall away. Shortly afterwards, new shoots that will produce next year's blossoms begin to spring up in their place. Meanwhile, the plant's roots and underground runners are developing in their own peculiar fashion. By autumn they split away from the old plant and colonize the area with new growth. The overall process is almost a vegetative version of the snake's renewing itself by splitting its skin.

Pomegranate Rose

[ROSA GALLICA GRANATA]

THIS VARIETY WAS NAMED by the French nurseryman Villemorin, who likened the color and size of its flowers to pomegranate fruits. This resemblance seems to have been the plant's outstanding feature; apparently, it was not sufficiently attractive to the average gardener, for this variety was rarely grown. Perhaps the fact that its blossoms were almost scentless didn't help its cause very much either. *Rosa gallica granata* flowered at the end of June, just in time to subject itself to intense competition. It seems not to have survived into modern times.

Sultana's Rose

[ROSA GALLICA MAHEKA]

WHEN CLAUDE ANTOINE THORY discussed this rose, he wrote something every botanical historian dreads to see: "The flower is so well known to everyone that nothing more need be said about it." As a result there is no information as to why this variety is called *maheka*. All that can be said is that the term represents a feminine noun or adjective, and there is a strong possibility that the name of a woman, country, island, or city is somehow involved. The common name of sultana's rose, though unscientific, does at least give us something understandable to go on in place of the nebulous botanical term.

Rosa gallica maheka seems to have been a product of the Dutch nurseries, and was introduced into France by André Dupont between 1800 and 1803. The French knew it as *Rose du serail,* rose of the harem, as well as by its other names, and they raised its doubled variety far more often than the single form shown by Thory. The distinguishing feature of the sultanas was the extraordinarily rich color of their petals, which deepened with full exposure to the sun.

Sulphur Rose

[ROSA HEMISPHAERICA]

ALL THE YELLOW ROSES of the world have one thing in common: each of them originated in the old kingdom of Persia. That fact, which should have simplified their history, has instead had the effect of obscuring it. First of all, medieval Persia was much larger than modern Iran and included what we now call Iraq, Afghanistan, and Soviet and Chinese Turkestan. Second, horticultural records were scarcely ever kept, although plants were transported from one end of Islam to the other—a region that stretched from Spain to the borders of China. The resulting historical confusion may never be straightened out. Nevertheless, we do know that in 756 A.D. the Emir Abd ar Rahman introduced yellow roses from Persia into his palace gardens at Cordoba. Moslem records from the fourteenth century also mention yellow roses; but Europe, outside of Moorish Spain, remained ignorant of them until the 1500s.

This species, *Rosa hemisphaerica,* was known earlier as *R. sulfurea*. It proved difficult to grow outside of southern Europe, for without plenty of dry heat its buds stayed closed, rotted, or sometimes split. English gardeners, because of the climate, rarely ever brought it into flower, but it was successfully raised in some French and German gardens. This rose is grown solely for its color; the blossoms have no scent whatever.

Portland Rose

[ROSA DAMASCENA COCCINEA]

IN 1800 THIS ROSE WAS NAMED for the Duchess of Portland, a famous rosarian of her time. It was regarded as a natural cross between the rose of four seasons and the rose of Provins, inheriting its dark red color from the latter species and its habit of recurring bloom from the former. Though there were claims that it produced a profusion of blossoms that lasted from July through October, those statements were somewhat exaggerated on both counts. Horticulture has always had its P. T. Barnums, as anyone who has ever seen a seed catalogue should know.

The Portland rose has a rather faint scent and is generally of a low-growing habit, about one to two feet high. Once considered among the finer roses, it now makes a less than impressive showing when compared with modern varieties. However, in 1812 the Portland rose produced a mutant variety, *Rose Lelieur,* which gained a place in rose history by becoming a parent of the hybrid everblooming roses (a term that somewhat exaggerates their performance). By 1814, when Louis XVIII was returned to the French throne, the name of the variety was changed to *Rose du roi* in his honor.

Noisette's Rose

[ROSA NOISETTIANA]

SOME REMINDERS OF the Old South live on in this rose, for it was developed in Charleston, S.C., in the early nineteenth century. A rice planter named Champney, whose hobby was growing roses, bred it in his garden by crossing *Rosa muscosa* and *R. chinensis*. He later gave cuttings to his friend, the nurseryman Philippe Noisette, who instantly recognized its horticultural value and requested permission to propagate it for the commercial market. Within a few years' time he was able to supply the south and had also sent cuttings to William Prince of Flushing, N.Y., through whose nursery, then the most important in America, the rose was soon distributed in the north.

Noisette also sent the plant to his brother Louis, whose nursery near Paris had formed the model for the Empress Josephine's garden at Malmaison. By 1820 the rose was grown throughout the milder parts of Europe; through its association with the Noisettes, it came to be called *Rosa noisettiana*.

A very fragrant rose that reaches eight to ten feet in height, it is unusually fertile for a hybrid, and is a parent of numerous varieties. As many as one hundred and thirty buds form in a kind of panicle at the ends of its branches and then come into bloom successively, from July until just before the first frost. Although hardy in the south, it needs winter protection in the north.

Blue Provins Rose

[ROSA GALLICA CAERULEA]

It took many years of patient breeding by Redouté to obtain this variety of rose in his garden at Fleury-sous-Meudon. From its petals, which are variegated dark and light rose, the latter spotted with touches of a deep pink, it seems likely that *Rosa gallica versicolor,* the striped apothecary's rose, and *R. gallica marmoreo,* the marbled rose, entered into its ancestry.

The name blue Provins rose comes not from its undeniably pink flowers but rather from its foliage, which has a pronounced bluish tint. The color, however, does not result so much from pigmentation as from an optical effect produced by the reflection of light from the surfaces of the leaflets. The same principle can be seen in iridescent oil films on puddles or in the plumage of some birds.

Specimens of the blue Provins rose were grown in the King's Flower Garden at Sèvres as well as by Redouté, but it was always rare. Few, if any, shrubs were ever raised on their own roots, for this variety succeeds better when grafted onto other root stocks. It requires a southern exposure, which indicates that it is somewhat tender, and needs winter protection.

Moss Rose

[ROSA CENTIFOLIA MUSCOSA]

THE FAMOUS OLD-FASHIONED moss rose is really not very old as roses go—a little less than three hundred years. Doubtlessly a mutant variety of *Rosa centifolia,* it first sprang up in southern France, in a region long noted for its many varieties of that species. Because it occasionally sheds its mossiness completely and reverts to the appearance of its parent stock, *Rosa centifolia muscosa* is considered a variety rather than a truly distinct species, although such model botanists as Willdenow and de Candolle mistakenly honored it with that designation early in the nineteeth century. According to Fréard du Castel, who was the first to document its origin, it had grown around the town of Carcassone since 1696.

The mossiness and stickiness of this rose come about because of numerous minute glands that cover the flower's stems and, very often, its leaflets. They also crowd the surfaces of its calyx, the cup-shaped form at the flower's base, and the sepals, the divided leaflike growths that surround its buds. Moss rose is low-growing, only two to three feet high, and does best in rich soil and high humidity. In June its rose-pink blossoms burst forth in profusion. Their aroma, which combines the scents of the cabbage rose and balsam, stems as much from its innumerable glands as from the blooms themselves. The original form of the variety is still preferable to all those developed later.

Chinese Rose

[ROSA CHINENSIS]

ALTHOUGH GOODS AND PLANTS had been imported sporadically from the Orient for hundreds of years, Europeans up to the eighteenth century rarely knew the source of anything they purchased. Their beloved and popular Bengal rose, then called *Rosa indica,* was entirely Chinese in origin, but that fact took 104 years to confirm. It was not until 1885, when Dr. Augustine Henry found the wild parent species growing in central China, that the ancestry of *Rosa chinensis,* as it is now known, could be determined. It had been patiently bred by the Chinese to its double form from a simple single-flowered species, *R. chinensis spontanea.* The Dutch were the first to have it in 1781, closely followed by the British and French, who bought it from them.

R. chinensis is an everblooming type, which inspired European gardeners to enthusiastic experiments with its hybridization. In its early days the lightness of its perfume and its tendency to freeze in hard winters were considered less important than its habit of repeated flowering. It also had another desirable characteristic: its color deepened rather than faded as the blossoms aged. Unluckily, its everblooming trait was not carried over to all its hybrid progeny, but some good did accrue, such as the production of the tea rose. It is also said to have provided the inspiration for Thomas Moore's ''The Last Rose of Summer,'' a logical tribute to its perpetual blossoming.

Tea Rose

[ROSA ODORATA]

In 1809, an agent of the East India Company passing through the port of Canton noticed *Rosa odorata* growing in a nearby nursery, and by 1810 specimens of it reached England. Unluckily, the early arrivals had poor and scanty flowers set on weak stems, and therefore aroused little interest. But when it became clear that this rose was closely related to *R. chinensis,* was everblooming, and could be obtained in a variety of forms and colors, the picture began to change. Crossbreeding of the two species soon got under way and completely altered the course of nineteenth-century rose culture, eventually producing well over a thousand varieties. Under the name *R. indica fragrans,* it came to America in 1828, and by 1831 enough specimens had been propagated to insure a steady supply to the trade.

R. odorata was once called the tea-scented rose because its scent resembles crushed, fresh tea leaves, and a shortened form of its name has carried over to its progeny, the hybrid tea roses. When it first appeared no one knows, but examples of it can be seen in Chinese paintings as far back as the tenth century. Although it needs protection from sudden changes of temperature, it is hardy and long-lived, and is easily propagated by rooting cuttings from it. Why this native of China was called Indian is a question, but its association with the East India Company may have brought about that error.

Apothecary's Rose

[ROSA GALLICA OFFICINALIS]

WHETHER THIS ROSE originated in France or in Asia Minor is a matter of debate that may never be settled. It is grown extensively throughout Europe and most particularly in France, where it is an important item of commerce in the pharmaceutical, perfume, liquor, and soap industries. It is sometimes called the Provins rose because it was chiefly grown around that town, about thirty-five miles south of Paris. When Marie Antoinette stopped there overnight in 1770 on her way to marry the Dauphin (later Louis XVI), the townspeople prepared for her a bed made entirely of rose blossoms.

Though we seldom consider the use of roses in modern medicine, this species does contain tannin, oils, sugar, wax, cyanin, and quercitin. It also has astringent, bactericidal, bile-removing, and anti-inflammatory properties. In medieval times roses were used to ease headaches, control vomiting, dysentery, and fever, heal wounds, and act as a restorative, a tonic for the liver, and as a mild laxative. While that may seem to be an exaggerated list, all of it is grounded in fact.

Rosa gallica officinalis is highly aromatic and has been appreciated for its scent and beauty since Roman times. It was among the prized plants brought to America by the Pilgrims, and naturalized readily in the New World. Its long, underground shoots make it almost impossible to eliminate once established. Empress Josephine was so fond of this rose and of all the gallica group that she had at least 167 varieties of them growing in her gardens at Malmaison, and about a thousand varieties were developed later in the nineteenth century, when gallicas were at the peak of their popularity.

Rose of Orléans

[ROSA GALLICA AURELIANENSIS]

ONE OF THE MOST BEAUTIFUL of all the French roses, this variety was dedicated by Redouté to the Duchesse d'Orléans. She was the wife of Louis Philippe Joseph d'Orléans, better known as Philippe-Egalité because of his democratic leanings. His role in the French Revolution earned him an honored spot on the guillotine in 1793, when the Revolution began to consume its own people. The Duchess, however, lived on until 1821 and gave France another of its kings, Louis Philippe, who reigned from 1830 to 1848. Since Redouté had lived through the same troublesome times as the Duchess, and had no doubt received her patronage, he took this means of honoring her.

The Latin term *aurelianensis* has nothing to do with the proper name Aurelia, but refers instead to the old Roman name for Orléans. The rose thus called grows from three to four feet high and is lightly and pleasantly scented. Its flowers are slow to develop and always appear late, extending the season of bloom by flowering after all the other roses are finished. The Orléans rose is seldom grown, though it is easy to raise, needing no more care than frequent sprinkling and a southern exposure. Perhaps its somewhat tardy habits are to blame for its neglect.

Thornless Rose

[ROSA FRANCOFURTANA INERMIS]

IT IS SOMEWHAT APPROPRIATE that a man called Muenchhausen was the first botanist to name this rose, since a thornless rose verges on the incredible—just like many of the mythical Baron Münchhausen's tales. Truth to tell, however, the "thornless" rose does have numerous very small prickles set just beneath the head of the flower, although the stem is indeed free of thorns. Both China and India were once credited with producing the rose, but its true place of origin turned out to be no more exotic than Switzerland.

Rosa francofurtana inermis is a hybrid from a natural cross between *R. gallica*, the French rose, and *R. cinnamomea*, the cinnamon rose. First described in 1583, it became known for its ease of cultivation and its ability to grow in any kind of soil. Its faintly fragrant blossoms are two to three inches wide and almost always solitary. They bloom at the beginning of May on shrubs that rise from four to five feet high. Because its fruits are similar in shape to turbans, the British horticulturist Aiton, who raised them at Kew, gave the rose its early scientific name of *R. turbinata*, which was later revised by Muenchhausen.

46

White Provence Rose

[ROSA CENTIFOLIA MUTABILIS]

ALTHOUGH THIS VARIETY is a true Provence rose, it originated not in France but in England, as the result of an accidental discovery made by an English nursery-man named Grimwood. Roses were his particular interest and he owned an extensive collection of them to which he added every year, journeying out into the countryside in search of new species and varieties. During one of Grimwood's annual excursions, in 1777, he passed through the town of Needham in Suffolk, and noticed this rose growing in a garden. When he asked its owner, one Mr. Richmond, for a cutting, he was surprised and delighted to be given the entire shrub. Richmond, the town baker, had himself received it from a ship's carpenter who had found it growing in a hedgerow near a house he was repairing, so it was a well-traveled plant by the time Grimwood got it home. In gratitude for the gift, he had the image of the rose engraved on a silver cup and sent it to Richmond, who kept it as a souvenir for the rest of his life.

Rosa centifolia mutabilis changes from bright pink when it first appears to flat white when fully open. Consequently, it earned the name black and white rose, and it has also been called snow centifolia.

Great Cabbage-leaved Rose

[ROSA CENTIFOLIA BULLATA]

THIS VARIETY OF ROSE is said to be a mutation that appeared for the first time in Holland in 1815. However, the first major horticultural journal in Europe, *Le Bon Jardinier* of Paris, mentions it in an issue dated 1813, so the flower's origin becomes debatable.

Sometimes called the crinkled, blistered, or lettuce rose because of the crumpled appearance of its leaves, it was propagated at Malmaison by André Dupont, founder of the Luxembourg Gardens. He and other early nineteenth-century horticulturists and botanists had been gathered at Malmaison by request of the Empress Josephine, and soon created the best and largest of all existing rose collections on its grounds. Josephine, it is said, held the world's first rose show there, basing it on the 250 species and varieties grown in her own gardens and greenhouses.

Few seeds of this or any other of the centifolia varieties manage to get pollinated because the overlapping petals of the flower hinder proper fertilization. However, once the central mass of petals is lifted out—with the stamens and pistils retained, of course—the difficulty is overcome, and the seeds will prove quite fertile. The leaves of *Rosa centifolia bullata*, in addition to their unusual thickness and surfaces, turn a deep bronze color in late summer. This trait and the sweet odor of its beautifully rounded blossoms have made it a longtime favorite among rose growers.

Perfumers' White Rose

[ROSA DAMASCENA BIFERA ALBA]

THIS VARIETY, TOGETHER with the pink perfumers' rose, always reached the Parisian flower markets well before the rose season began. Starting in 1785, the nurserymen of the region instituted a system of forcing growth that assured an early and ample supply of roses at the end of winter, just when people were most anxious to see a touch of color.

This white variety is more delicate than its pink counterpart, and is not as dependably recurrent in its blooming habits. Neither is it pure white in color; it preserves a hint of pale blush in its pleasantly scented petals. Good soil and a favorable exposure are essential to its growth, and it is generally grafted onto roots of the dog rose to promote vigor and a beautiful effect of abundant bloom. The grafts, however, must be renewed periodically on new root stock in order to preserve the effect. Modern hybridization practices have eliminated many such botherations and uncertainties from rose growing by producing improved varieties, giving twentieth-century gardeners fewer difficulties.

Queen Elizabeth's Eglantine

[ROSA EGLANTERIA ZABETH]

FOLLOWING AN OLD ENGLISH tradition that associated this rose with Good Queen Bess, André Dupont used an abbreviation of "Elizabeth" in naming the variety. A low-growing plant, this eglantine gives off the pleasing scent (especially strong after it rains) of the old-fashioned pippin apple, which is not altogether surprising since roses and apples are members of the same family. The leaves, rather than the flowers, create the perfume, and it may be noticed even before there are any blossoms on the shrubs.

The true eglantines produce large quantities of seeds, almost all of which germinate, and they readily accept pollen from other roses. The result is an almost endless number of varieties growing in the wild. When these hybrids are brought into cultivation, however, and self-pollinate, they promptly drop their hybrid characteristics and become pure eglantines again. This tendency made it difficult to stabilize the qualities that nurserymen bred into them until the end of the nineteenth century.

Queen Elizabeth's eglantine closely resembles *Rosa eglanteria hessoise*, one of the most popular roses in nineteenth-century France. It is still available, but *R. eglanteria zabeth* appears to be out of cultivation. It may have survived somewhere, however, because eglantines send out numerous underground shoots, and can thus propagate themselves for centuries in a limited area.

Dawn Damask Rose

[ROSA DAMASCENA AURORA]

THIS ROSE HAS A twofold claim on the name of dawn damask. The color of its petals is like that of the sky just as rosy dawn breaks; and it was named for a young Polish lady, Aurora Poniatowska, the daughter of one of Thory's special friends. She was also among Redouté's best pupils, one who he hoped would carry the art of flower painting back to Poland with her.

Of Dutch origin, this variety of damask rose was propagated in France at the Luxembourg and Malmaison gardens by André Dupont. He apparently created enough shrubs to satisfy the nursery trade, for it was listed in nearly every nineteenth-century catalogue; but somehow or other, amateur gardeners seemed unaware of it, and it was seldom grown in French gardens. This neglect is all the more puzzling in light of the rose's undeniable beauty and ability to flourish when grafted onto eglantine root stock. Thory quite rightly considered it one of the finest varieties to cultivate.

Seven Sisters Rose

[ROSA MULTIFLORA PLATYPHYLLA]

WHOLE PLANTS OF THIS ROSE arrived safely in London from China in 1815, which was something of a miracle in those days, when most live plants perished during the customary long ocean voyages. Two years later, the same species was found on the grounds of a London market gardener, who had raised them from seeds he had received from Japan. In 1819 they finally reached France, where cuttings from the London-grown roses were planted and thrived.

For many years, this species of multiflora was cultivated in greenhouses and orangeries while a gradual program of acclimatization was undertaken. When specimens were finally set fully out of doors, in 1826, they proved hardy enough to survive the very hard winter of that year. Nonetheless it is still advisable to treat it as a tender climber.

One difficulty in maintaining this rose stems from its rather thin and easily damaged bark. Its tissues often suffer severe disruption when the branches are soaked with rain and then exposed to an abrupt drop in temperature. Part of the trouble lies in its habit of producing vigorous growth late in the summer, a timing that leaves the plant highly susceptible to winter damage.

Rosa multiflora platyphylla is cultivated in the same way as the bramble rose, on roots of the eglantine. It produces clusters of eight to thirty blossoms, pink to mauve in color, varying in the size and quantity of their petals.

Creamy Musk Rose

[ROSA STYLOSA LEUCOCHROA]

THIS ROSE PROBABLY HAD the musk rose, *Rosa moschata*, as one of its parents, but nothing more can be determined about its ancestry. It grew six to eight feet high, bearing yellowish-white flowers of a light, pleasant odor similar to that of the musk rose. Its height, aroma, and characteristically short styles (the threadlike necks of the blossoms' ovaries) all suggest a very close relationship to *R. moschata*.

The creamy musk rose grew in Poitou and Anjou, western provinces of France, but was rarely found elsewhere in the early nineteenth century. There seems to be no modern record of the variety, so it probably did not survive the competition it met once it entered cultivation. There are fashions in roses just as there are in clothes, and though species persist, varieties and hybrids come and go with the changing tastes of the times.

Cottony Rose

[ROSA TOMENTOSA MULTIPLICI]

THIS MEMBER OF THE DOG ROSE group has been vastly improved by cultivation, which has increased both the size of the blooms and the quantity of their petals. It is derived from the wild woodland rose, *Rosa tomentosa,* which grew in profusion in the forest of Fontainebleau near Paris at the beginning of the nineteenth century. There, however, its blossoms were of the single type.

In 1817 a double variety of *R. tomentosa* was found growing in the woods at Meudon, nearby the home of the artist Redouté. There his daughter, Josephine, discovered them in an area preserved as a pheasantry for autumn shooting.

This rose reaches a height of four to five feet, and usually bears its faintly aromatic flowers in groups of three. It requires a cool, shady location, hence its preference for a woodland location, and blooms in late June. Its common name, the cottony rose, comes from the not very obvious fact that the interiors of its calices, the cups beneath the flowers, have a felt-like lining very much like white cotton.

Great Maiden's Blush Rose

[ROSA ALBA INCARNATA]

Since this is a rather conspicuous rose, it was inevitable that it would be known by more than one name. Among the highly appropriate terms for it are the great, the virginal, great maiden's blush, royal white, carnation, and—as might be expected from the royal French courts that admired such allusions— nymph's thigh.

Rosa alba incarnata first received botanical mention in 1557 by the English herbalist and cleric Dr. William Turner, although it had been known well before his day. As so often happens with roses from earlier times, when records were haphazard at best, the origin of this rose has been lost; it is presumed to be a cross between *R. canina* and either *R. damascena* or *R. gallica*. It is found in several places throughout Europe, but, of course, with no certainty as to which area it is native to, if any.

The great maiden's blush grows about five feet high, bearing three-inch flowers which have a tendency to stay closed. Their aroma is reminiscent of white hyacinths. Left to its own devices in a garden, this rose reverts from its very double form to a single one with seven to eight petals, indicating that the double form is a garden variety.

Leafy Cabbage Rose

[ROSA CENTIFOLIA FOLIACEA]

WHILE THIS VARIETY has leaflets of rather large size, it is not for the foliage that it is named. It is rather because the sepals, which more or less unite to form the green cuplike calyx that covers the base of the flower, are so lengthened that they look like leaves. Actually, the sepals *are* modifications of leaves—just as are the thorns, calyx, petals, pistil, and stamens. In fact, the numerous extra petals found in all double varieties of roses are nothing more than modified stamens, and are thus modifications of a modification.

The sepals of *Rosa centifolia foliacea* are so deeply divided that they nearly fail to form a calyx at all. The exaggerated leaflike shapes they form rise up about the bud so as to make a coronet, giving this variety a very distinct appearance. The rose can only be propagated by grafting or layering, and thrives best when set upon understocks of *R. canina*. In the area of St. Denis, where many Parisian nurserymen once had their gardens, this variety was successfully grown for many years. It is probably no longer available commercially, but may reappear at any time as either a mutation or a variation of some closely related centifolia.

Turpentine Rose

[ROSA VILLOSA TEREBINTHINA]

THIS VARIETY OF ROSE is more remarkable for its curious features than for traditionally attractive ones. First of all, it has extremely large leaflets which exude a very strong scent of turpentine, and it is difficult to reconcile the smell of a paint factory with that of a garden. Second, it prefers to be grown in the shade; for that reason, it was once used to ornament English parks and gardens, where large shade trees were in plentiful supply. If grown in full sun, its foliage is much less vigorous—which might prove advantageous in regard to its odor.

The flowers of the turpentine rose have almost no scent whatever. It is a hybrid of *Rosa canina,* but, despite that hardy ancestral stock, it is now rare and may be horticulturally extinct.

Purple Velvet Rose

[ROSA GALLICA PURPUREA VELUTINA]

THIS MAGNIFICENT VARIETY was developed in Van Eden's nurseries at Haarlem, the Netherlands, and was presented to Empress Josephine by the Dutch entrepreneur in 1810. It attracted widespread attention as soon as it came into her gardens at Malmaison, fueling the already intense interest in all varieties of the gallicas. At that time over five hundred varieties were being grown in France and the Netherlands, a figure that would rise to one thousand before the nineteenth century ended.

The petals of the purple velvet rose are very double, and their lively, deep reddish-purple reflects varying tints of violet according to the changing angle of light. That somewhat iridescent quality was beyond the skill of painters to capture—even Redouté himself, as Thory mentions in his description of this rose. Moreover, as the flow of sap diminishes in the petals, just before they fall, they turn a very dark color—so deep that the flower is sometimes called the black rose.

After Josephine's death in 1814, this variety disappeared from Malmaison, but was later recovered from grafted specimens growing in gardens at Fleury. Generally, however, it is grown on its own roots, which was Van Eden's method, and does better if left somewhat to its own devices.

Thornless Alsatian Rose

[R O S A   S P I N O S I S S I M A   I N E R M I S]

THIS ROSE IS NATIVE to the Vosges Mountains, which lie near the Franco-German border. It was found growing close to the Alsatian landmark known as Champ de Feu, or field of fire, midway between Nancy and Strasbourg. Its discoverer, one Monsieur Nestler, immediately sent a specimen to the Swiss botanist Augustin de Candolle, who confirmed that it was a new species.

The simplicity of the thornless rose adds greatly to its appeal. Its flowers are of the single type, and its five large petals, almost white at their centers, are bordered with a band of dark pink on their outer edges. The plant grows about three feet high, and while its branches are still young they may have many small, slight thorns. However, they shrink as the branch matures, and by flowering time they will have disappeared. Little care is needed in raising this variety other than placing it where it will get plenty of sun. Once popular, it now seems to be out of commercial supply; but true enthusiasts can always gather their own while abroad.

Clustered Marsh Rose

[ROSA PALUSTRIS SUBCORYMBOSA]

THERE ARE EXCEPTIONS to every iron-clad rule, and the statement that "Every rose has its thorn" is one of them. Not a single one of the marsh roses, including this one, has ever so armed itself, and there is even a variety of the thorny rose which has no thorns at all.

The gardeners who raised this rose at Malmaison and at Auteuil, where the pleasure garden of Monsieur Ternaux provided this specimen for Redouté's brush, apparently placed it in ordinary soil. Had they put it in a marshy situation—which they probably couldn't—it would undoubtedly have grown well over the two to three feet it attained in a relatively dry setting. This variety is distinguished by the flower clusters at its branch tips.

White Rose of Fleury

[ROSA ALBA FOLIACEA]

IT IS A DISTINCT POSSIBILITY that this rose was developed in Redouté's garden at Fleury-sous-Meudon. Thory mentions it as a new variety in his time, and expected it to be more highly valued by gardeners once it became better known. Since Redouté rarely exhibited his roses, or any other of his flowers, Thory's reticence about whose garden it grew in is probably a reflection of Redouté's own attitude.

The particular instance to which Thory refers was the first time this rose had been grown from seed and brought into flower. That may very well indicate the end result of a long program of breeding, since this tender variety was always propagated elsewhere by means of grafting.

The white rose of Fleury blooms in early spring and has a sweet fragrance. Its pure matte white flowers, more than three inches wide, are carried on stems that are bristly just below the calices, though elsewhere they are almost free of thorns. Somewhat tender, the plant needs shelter in the winter. The bushes grow about three feet high, a good, average height. If Redouté was truly responsible for breeding it, his reputation could only be enhanced thereby; but he may have been unaccountably shy about such things.

Carolina Rose

[ROSA CAROLINA]

Rosa Carolina is native to North America and is a true species with many varieties, which seem to result from the various local conditions found in its huge area of distribution. It grows from eastern Canada to Florida and from Texas to Wisconsin; and because it has adapted to the widely differing environments in that swath of territory it has to be considered an extremely hardy rose. Iowa has named it the state flower (despite its connection to the Carolinas), which is testimony that this rose is made of very stern stuff— strong enough to withstand Midwestern winters.

The blossoms of *R. carolina* are about two inches wide with a light and pleasant fragrance, and are borne in June on shrubs rising five to six feet tall. The plant has an air of elegance with its clear, rose-colored flowers carried gracefully in clusters of three to six. In Paris it has been reported to bloom two months later than in America.

R. carolina will hybridize with the cinnamomea and spinosissima roses but generally resists any attempt to breed it with other species. For some reason its seeds, unlike those of other roses, are held only in the bottoms of its fruits. This is of no observable advantage to the plant, though it may be a factor in its reluctance to crossbreed.

Perfumers' Rose

[ROSA DAMASCENA BIFERA OFFICINALIS]

THIS VERY FRAGRANT ROSE was the flower most used by French perfumers through the nineteenth century. It commonly blooms twice a year, in June and November; hence the Latin term *bifera,* or twice-yielding, in its scientific name. Very old roots, planted at the Tuileries in Paris, were observed to blossom throughout the year, and thus it earned the name rose of four seasons. Ordinarily it flowers in June and November.

As early as 1785, the perfumers' rose was grown commercially to provide cut flowers for city markets in France. Quite possibly, the great sixteenth-century French essayist Michel Montaigne was indirectly responsible for the appearance of *R. damascena bifera officinalis* in France. He introduced the damask rose, which has long been considered its parent, into his native southwestern France on returning from Italy. Montaigne's region has always been the presumed area of origin for the perfumers' rose, and there are times when tradition is almost as trustworthy as documents—sometimes more so.

Austrian Yellow Rose

[R O S A   F O E T I D A]

SHAKESPEARE TO THE CONTRARY, this rose by any name refuses to smell sweet. Whether it is called the Austrian yellow, Austrian brier, yellow sweetbrier, or yellow eglantine, it remains steadfast in the production of a disagreeable odor. Its origin is Asiatic, either Turkey or old Persia, though some horticulturists erroneously ascribed it to Austria and others to the environs of Paris.

Rosa foetida was introduced into Spain by the Moors during the thirteenth century, from whence it was gradually distributed throughout the rest of Europe. It spread rather slowly at first because it produced very few seeds, its cuttings rarely ever rooted, and its subterranean suckers (growths by which many kinds of roses propagate themselves) were scarce in this species. Those difficulties of cultivation have now been overcome through the techniques of budding and grafting.

The shrub grows from eight to ten feet high or more, and its jonquil-yellow flowers provide an attractive splash of color in June. Its fresh leaves have a pleasant aroma, making up for the ill-scented flowers. Some advantages in raising it are that it needs almost no care and seems to prefer poor soils to good ones. On the other hand, it soon overruns any arbor it is meant to cover, and dislikes the pruning operations needed to keep it under control.

Cugnot's Rose

[ROSA SEPIUM FLORE SUBMULTIPLICI]

THE TERM *sepium,* which means in or of hedges, is obsolete in the modern nomenclature of roses. Moreover, the gardener who raised this rose, one Monsieur Cugnot, neglected to give it a common name, leaving no choice but to call it after him. He also failed to leave a record of its ancestry. The result is a horticultural fog of considerable density, and whether this flower should be classed as a species, a variety, or a hybrid may remain an open question. All the solid evidence we have lies in Redouté's illustration of a rose that no longer exists, and that has its obvious limitations.

In 1629, John Parkinson described a double variety of eglantine rose very similar to this one, but it had only ten petals, whereas Cugnot's rose had twenty or more. The variety Parkinson spoke of had occurred naturally, so there is every chance that nature may have redoubled the number of petals in the two hundred years between Parkinson's description and the time Cugnot brought his own variety into flower. There is, however, the possibility that Cugnot may simply have crossed an eglantine with something else, producing a hybrid rather than a variety. Since hybrids are often infertile, the rose could have easily disappeared. Whatever the case, we have Redouté's drawing as a souvenir, which is always in bloom and needs neither pruning nor care.

Celery-leaved Rose

[ROSA CENTIFOLIA BIPINNATA]

THIS ROSE, though highly fragrant, is not grown for its flowers, which are very similar to those of the common hundred-leaved or cabbage rose. Instead the plant is valued for its unusual foliage, which has crisped, curled edges very much like those of celery, parsley, or gooseberries. It is propagated by the technique of layering, which involves rooting the tips of branches still attached to the parent plant. This procedure is necessary because the variety will not always breed true from seed. The French horticulturist Dupont is said to have overcome that difficulty in the 1820s, but he also noted that it was slow to raise from seed.

The celery-leaved rose is a low shrub, about one and a half feet high. Once started, it is then best continued on the roots of *Rosa canina,* the dog rose, where it will grow vigorously. Apparently it prefers a little benign neglect; too much care, as one nineteenth-century French gardener observed, often caused the most flourishing specimens to perish. Even when all the rules are respected, it still tends to revert to its original form, with ordinary leaves. Small wonder that it almost became extinct in gardens before Dupont tamed it.

Cherokee Rose

[ROSA LAEVIGATA]

THIS TRAILING OR CLIMBING ROSE, which can produce stems fifty feet long—covering more than ten thousand square feet—from a single, undisturbed growth, is one of the great mysteries of the plant kingdom. It is of Chinese origin, having been grown there for centuries, and was brought back to Europe in 1794 by Lord Macartney, England's first diplomatic representative to Peking. At about the same time, however, the French botanical explorer André Michaux discovered it growing in the southern United States in Georgia, where it has since become the state flower. Later explorations revealed that it ranged as far west as the Mississippi, and it became obvious that the rose had been established here centuries before any Europeans had arrivzd. The question of how it got here, if ever answered, may someday provide very interesting data for pre-Columbian historians.

The three-inch-wide flowers of the cherokee rose, to give it its common American name, have no scent but are of a pure snowy white color. That fact caused it to be called *Rosa nivea,* the snow-white rose, before it was named *R. laevigata.* It prefers a slightly moist soil, somewhat enriched with manure. It also likes a southern climate and will not bloom in the north, although it will survive there. It cannot be crossed easily with other roses, nor succeed well when grafted onto other roots. Its finicky, exclusive habits make it even more difficult to understand how this rose ever traveled so far.

Malmédy Rose

[ROSA CANINA MALMUNDARIENSIS]

ONCE THOUGHT TO BE A VARIETY of *Rosa montana,* this rose proved instead to be one of the dog roses—which have more virtues than their common name implies. The term came about because dog rose fruits were valued in the ancient world as a cure for rabies induced by dog bite. In addition, they are a proven major source of Vitamin C, and also contain Vitamins A, B_1, B_2, and K. They are useful in treating gall, kidney, and bladder stones, as a diuretic, and in the relief of coughs and intestinal rheum as well.

This variety, *R. canina malmundariensis,* which is simply Latin for the dog rose of Malmédy, was found in the mountains near that Belgian town. It rises some six or seven feet high, and bears blossoms either in solitary fashion or by twos or threes. The rose is noted for its very large fruits, also called hips.

The Malmédy rose was discovered by one Dr. Le Jeune, who was a French physician and botanist—a very frequent combination in the nineteenth century. He compiled a list of all the plants that grew around the neighboring health resort of Spa, and it is more than likely that he treated patients there while pursuing his botanical interests in his off hours. Spa, of course, was the great eighteenth- and nineteenth-century watering place whose name is now synonymous with other such resorts the world over.

Turnip Rose

[ROSA VIRGINIANA PLENA]

BESIDES ITS NAME OF turnip rose, this variety of the Virginian rose is also known by the more attractive ones of *Rose d'amour*, St. Mark's rose, and the ash-leaved rose. It was first brought under cultivation in the American colonies in 1724, and began to be grown in European gardens in 1768.

The turnip rose reaches heights of about five feet, and bears very double flowers with four to five rows of petals. The blossoms, however, are produced slowly and often prove abortive. Another peculiarity of the variety is that while the flowering branches of this shrub are almost entirely free of thorns, the older branches always develop a few. Perhaps another name might be based on its tardy habits, such as "slow starter" or the "late, late rose."

Anemone Rose

[ROSA CENTIFOLIA ANEMONOIDES]

IN 1800 A FRENCH NURSERYMAN named Poilpré discovered this rose growing in the fields around his home in Mans. A neighbor, the Chevalier de Tascher, identified it as a new variety of the hundred-leaved rose; at the same time, it resembled an anemone, and so he called it *Rosa centifolia anemonoides*. Poilpré sold it under that name for many years afterwards.

How the anemone rose ever developed spontaneously in the wild is something of a mystery, for it cannot be propagated in cultivation except by grafting onto hardier stock or by rooting the tips of its branches. It had to have been a natural cross between the ordinary *R. centifolia* and *R. lheritieranea;* but since the centifolias are notoriously poor producers of fertile seeds, there were heavy odds against its creation from the very first. Nonetheless, the miracle happened, and a beautiful new variety came into being.

R. centifolia anemonoides is a tender, low-growing shrub, about two feet high. It needs a sheltered spot in the garden, and should be pruned at the end of February. If it is exposed to rigorous weather, the result will be either very few flowers or a very dead shrub.

Bramble Rose

[ROSA MULTIFLORA CARNEA]

IN 1804, THOMAS EVANS of the English East India Company brought this rose back from China to England, and it flowered a few years later in the London nurseries of the Messrs. Colville. From there it traveled to France in 1808, and was eventually distributed throughout western Europe by 1817.

Probably a natural hybrid of *Rosa chinensis* and *R. multiflora cathayensis*, *R. multiflora carnea* has since entered into the parentage of many varieties of the multifloras, polyanthas, and floribundas, species whose names all mean many-flowered. The shrub, a climbing variety, puts forth a profusion of bloom in late May or early June, and produces even greater abundance when grafted onto roots of the eglantine rose.

While the bramble rose, to give it its English name, will adapt to many different soils and growing conditions, it is only moderately hardy and requires shelter in the winter. Great numbers of this shrub, many of which had been trained over arbors and latticework in open places, were destroyed in the ice storms that swept over Paris in November and December of 1812. The French gardens then experienced a touch of the same conditions Napoleon met with in Russia during that fateful year.

Marsh Rose

[ROSA PALUSTRIS]

THIS ROSE WAS originally named in honor of Henry Hudson, who discovered the great Canadian bay where this species grows naturally. It is not confined to that area, however, but ranges south to Florida and west as far as Iowa, being generally found in marshy areas. *Rosa palustris,* as both its common and botanical names indicate, is fond of very wet soil, and will grow to eight feet or more in such locations. In dry soil, to which it can adapt if necessary, it takes on a dwarfed aspect, growing as a shrub no more than two feet high.

Because of its long and rather slender and lengthy foliage, *R. palustris* was once termed the willow leaf rose, and it is often confused with the closely related Carolina rose. The marsh rose has clusters of deep pink blossoms, which appear at intervals from June to August. It was very common in French nurseries in the early nineteenth century, having been under cultivation since 1726. Easily raised from seed, it attains its flowering state in three years, and needs almost no care. However, its habit of propagating by means of underground shoots results in a tendency to spread. Roses that are easy to grow are almost always hard to keep under control.

Austrian Copper Rose

[ROSA FOETIDA BICOLOR]

THIS VARIETY OF *Rosa foetida* has a vague early history, and all evidence points to its being a mutation. Occasionally *R. foetida* and *R. foetida bicolor* can be found springing from the same root, which should settle all questions of origin. The variety presents a great deal of color variation, running from pure yellow—the color of its parent species—through orange, copper, and pomegranate red. Sometimes the petals have stripes of a purplish hue, which led to its being called tulip rose, after the broken colored tulips so popular in the eighteenth century. It was also known in England as the pomegranate eglantine, although the blossoms of a true eglantine are always pink or white.

Rosa foetida bicolor is as easy to cultivate as its parent, needing little care and thriving in poor soil as well as or better than in good. Its flowers are much less offensive in smell than those of *R. foetida*, but by the same token the pleasant aroma of the foliage is rather weaker in this variety.

Soft Rose

[ROSA MOLLIS]

THE LEAFLETS OF THIS ROSE are covered with a multitude of extremely fine hairs that give one's fingertips the sensation of stroking a very soft, almost velvety fabric. It is of compact growth, quite hardy, and may be found throughout Europe and western Asia. Its favorite sites are hillsides and thickets.

Because of its ample foliage and deep pink blossoms, which are almost fully double, *Rosa mollis* is a most desirable shrub for the pleasure garden. One of its special conveniences is the near absence of thorns on the new growth that produces the flowers. Cultivation alters it very little, and it needs scarcely more attention than trimming away its dead wood. A member of the dog rose group, the soft rose appears to have been derived from *R. rubrifolia,* the red-leaved rose, and *R. pendulina,* the pendant rose—so called because of the way it carries its fruits.

Cumberland Rose

[ROSA CENTIFOLIA ANGLICA RUBRA]

THE COMMON NAME OF Cumberland rose would seem to indicate that this rose was native to the lake country of northwestern England, but that is by no means a certainty. John Parkinson, the herbalist of Jacobean and Carolean times, referred to it in 1629 as *Rosa anglica rubra,* the red rose of England, and said that it was an ancient insignia of the English kings, long known and used medicinally throughout England. Nonetheless, it may very well have been introduced from Italy by the Romans at an even earlier time.

The Cumberland rose was introduced into France at the beginning of the nineteenth century and soon gained popularity in French gardens. Its very fragrant flowers, growing on bushes about two feet high, made it desirable as a low border hedge, but the plant was somewhat tender in cold regions. Its leaves are quite soft to touch, a characteristic of the true centifolia roses. However, its petals differ from those of the ordinary centifolia, which deepen their color nearer to the heart of the flower; those of the Cumberland rose remain uniformly colored from circumference to center. There seems to be no modern record of the variety having been kept in cultivation, but wild specimens or garden escapees must still exist wherever the rose was once grown.

Bell Rose

[ROSA FRANCOFURTANA CAMPANULATA]

ONCE CONSIDERED A full-fledged species, this rose was finally determined to be only a variety of the Frankfort rose. It is but faintly fragrant, and was chiefly used for bordering hedges, since it grows no more than about two feet high. The name bell rose refers to its bell-shaped calices, rather than to its flowers.

Its principal horticultural interest is in its coloration, which is white with only the slightest tinge of rose in its center. All other varieties of the Frankfort rose range from light pink to deep red, so this is the only white rose of its group.

At the beginning of the nineteenth century, the leading nurserymen and gardeners of the Parisian area all grafted this rose onto root stocks of other species. Only one breeder, Monsieur Cugnot, managed to raise it from seed. As a hybrid, its seeds were probably not very fertile, and propagation would generally come about through vegetative techniques or grafting. There seems to be no recent record of this variety, so it may now be extinct.

Climbing Marsh Rose

[ROSA PALUSTRIS SCANDENS]

As ONE WOULD EXPECT of a rose that came directly into cultivation from the wild, this variety can be grown quite easily from seed. The Latin term *scandens*, which means climbing, is appropriate for this variety of the marsh rose, which can twine up over any support it can find and will soon cover any arbor or pergola.

The branches of the climbing marsh rose become reddish-brown when exposed to sunlight; they are thornless, as is the case with other roses of this species. The flowers are borne in solitary fashion, and make a most attractive display with their bicolored blossoms, whose petals are alternately light and dark rose. *Rosa palustris scandens* blooms in May, and does best in a moist soil. When raised from seed, it will flower in the third year.

De Candolle's Rose

[ROSA SPINOSISSIMA CANDOLLEANA]

THIS VARIETY OF THE Scotch or burnet Rose, now classed as one of the spinosis-simas, was considered for a time to be a separate species. On further examination, however, it proved to be simply another variation of the very thorny rose as the term *spinosissima* indicates.

As a shrub it is elegant and graceful in shape, which inspired its early name, *Rosa candolleana elegans*. It was then intended to honor the Swiss botanist Augustin Pyramus de Candolle (1778–1841), whose system of classification —devised before Darwin's theories of evolution were ever formulated— vastly improved the science of botany. In fact, much of de Candolle's work survived that unforeseen storm to enter into modern botanical usage.

Rosa spinosissima candolleana is a highly fragrant shrub that rises from four to five feet high. Like other spinosissimas, which have an enormous range throughout Europe and temperate Asia, it will often grow where many other roses will not. The species is highly variable in gardens, and this variety may no longer even exist, for there is no modern mention of it.

Single-flowered Cinnamon Rose

[ROSA CINNAMOMEA FLORE SIMPLICI]

CINNAMON ROSES ARE ALL highly variable; apparently their color is not dictated by their genes, but depends upon the kind of soil and situation in which they grow. The red color of this variety, the single-flowered cinnamon rose, varies in intensity according to the kind of soil it finds itself in.

Rosa cinnamomea flore simplici, an attractive shrub of medium height, springs up spontaneously in fields throughout all of southern Europe, but is not confined to that area. It can, in fact, be found thriving everywhere from western Europe to Japan. It blooms, as do most roses, in the month of June, bearing two-toned pink petals. Originally a wild rose, it has long since found its way into the domestic garden.

York and Lancaster Rose

[ROSA DAMASCENA VERSICOLOR]

THE NAME *Rosa damascena versicolor* could very easily be interpreted as the versatile damask in the case of this rose. Normally it displays petals striped red and white, combining the colors of the English houses of Lancaster and York. On some occasions, however, a single shrub will outdo itself and present solid red and white blossoms along with the striped ones.

Because of its red (actually pink) and white petals, this variety is sometimes confused with *Rosa mundi*, which is not a damask but rather one of the French roses. A Spanish physician, Nicolas Monardes of Seville, was the first to describe it when he wrote on the medical properties of roses in the sixteenth century. Aside from that verifiable fact, almost everything else about the York and Lancaster rose is a subject of controversy. Most of the legends about its history trace back to Shakespeare and are of no documentary value.

The shrub was widely grown in England both before and after Elizabethan times, but curiously enough, the famous herbalist of that era, John Gerard, makes no mention of it in his herbal. Gerard had often been accused of plagiarizing the work of Rembert Dodoens, a Flemish botanist, who also failed to mention the York and Lancaster rose. Whether coincidence or copying was responsible for Gerard's omission is a decision that readers will have to make for themselves.

Rose of Love

[ROSA GALLICA PUMILA]

HERE IS A ROSE that totally ignored political boundaries, as does everything else in nature. It grew spontaneously in all parts of Germany, although it was supposedly French; yet for some reason, the Germans never troubled to claim it, but instead called it the rose of Austria. Perhaps that name may indicate its place of origin; but, as with many roses, its history remains an enigma.

As the Latin word *pumila* signifies, this variety of *Rosa gallica* is a low-growing dwarf shrub, generally less than two feet high. It is, however, very fragrant, bearing its blossoms either singly or by twos and threes at the tips of its stems.

The French have their own common name for this rose, much the best of all of them: rose of love. Farmers who have to contend with its rampant growth don't speak of it as tenderly, though, for it can reappear and multiply almost as rapidly as it is uprooted from their farmland. Its proliferation is three-pronged: through selfsown seeds, offshoots (which act in much the same way as artificial layering), and subterranean roots. As a triple threat to agriculturists, it gets little love from them, but the rest of us do enjoy it.

Redouté's Rose

[R O S A   N I T I D A   R E D U T E A]

WHEN CLAUDE ANTOINE THORY was writing *Les Roses*, he wanted to honor his artist, Pierre-Joseph Redouté, in the book. With that in mind, he named a recently discovered rose *Rosa redutea glauca* and felt confident that all was well. Unluckily for Thory, his choice turned out to be a poor one, for not only was his variety name invalidated, but the plant itself seems to have dropped out of cultivation.

The rose was actually a variety of *Rosa nitida*, an American species found in 1807, but Thory imagined it to be a cross between the burnet rose, *R. spinosissima*, and the red-leaved rose, *R. rubrifolia*. There seems, however, no reason for his having wrenched Redouté's name out of joint by removing the letter "o" while Latinizing it. Nor does the term *glauca*, which Thory used in forming his botanical name, make much sense. Translated from the Latin, it means light sea-green, and refers here only to the upper surfaces of the leaves—hardly the best way to identify the plant. Even though this variety seems to have vanished, no book on Redouté's roses would be complete without it. In any case, although Thory's wish to honor Redouté came to naught, it was a good intention and deserves some recognition here.

Carnation Rose

[ROSA CENTIFOLIA CARYOPHYLLEA]

ROSA CENTIFOLIA has always had a tendency to mutate, and practically every one of its early varieties was the result of that natural process, including the carnation rose. The centifolias generally produced few seeds, and those that they did were rarely fertilized because the numerous petals nearly sealed in the pistils and stamens. Since artificial pollination was not in vogue before the nineteenth century, most rose varieties occurred spontaneously and were propagated by means of cuttings and graftings. *R. centifolia caryophyllea* was found by chance in a garden at Mantes-sur-Seine in 1800, and was later conserved at the Luxembourg Gardens in Paris by grafting and budding.

When grafted onto the roots of eglantine roses, this variety flourished and produced an abundance of flowers, though the shrubs, which always tended to revert rather easily, had to be renewed from time to time. The original shrub on which the carnation rose first appeared was found to have degenerated, and that is probably what induced the mutation. While the carnation rose was widely available from nineteenth-century French nurseries, there is no modern record of it, so it may have disappeared from cultivation.

Great Double White Rose

[ROSA ALBA FLORE PLENA]

I<small>T IS QUITE POSSIBLE</small> that one of the ancient names for England, Albion, was given to it by the Romans because of the many white roses found there. But whether or not the *Rosa alba* group was present then is quite another question, for the albas are natural hybrids that were formed in an unknown place at an unknown time. It has been guessed that they resulted from a cross between the dog rose and either the damask or the French rose. But whatever the ancestry of the great double white rose, we can be thankful that it *did* come along.

Since this variety grows six to ten feet high, it is very suitable for forming enclosures, and was commonly used for that purpose in the hedgerows and vineyards around Wurtzburg during the eighteenth and nineteenth centuries. The great double white also figured in many paintings of the Italian Renaissance. Its blossoms, which have an odor similar to white hyacinths, are faintly buff-colored at first but become white when fully open.

Virginian Rose

[ROSA VIRGINIANA]

ROSA VIRGINIANA WAS the first major American rose to be introduced into the gardens of Europe. It was brought to England in 1724 and soon gained great popularity there as well as on the Continent. Far from being confined to Virginia, as its name indicates, it ranges from Quebec to Missouri and southwards to Georgia. The original name, *R. lucida*, was more accurately descriptive of the species since it means shining, a term well suited to its nearly translucent petals and glistening foliage.

The lightly aromatic blossoms are borne in clusters of three or four at the ends of the stems. They flower in June in a sunny, southern exposure; should you wish to extend the flowering season, however, place the plant in shade, and it will not bloom until August or September. Individual blossoms are short-lived but quickly replace themselves. The shrub will grow about five to six feet high in good, light soil. It is of ornamental interest through much of the gardening year; the canes become reddish brown in the fall, when the leaves turn, and the bright red, globular fruits often persist into wintertime.

Cels's Damask Rose

[R O S A   D A M A S C E N A   C E L S I A N A]

WHILE THIS VARIETY SEEMS to have originated in eighteenth-century Holland, it was Jacques Martin Cels who introduced it into France and made it popular there; hence his friend and associate Thory named it in Cels's memory. It bears delightfully scented blossoms, about three inches wide, which have a curious habit of being soft rose in color when they first open and then turning almost white. The blooms are produced in great numbers and are found in various stages of coloration on one bush at the same time, producing the effect of a bicolored shrub. Shade will lengthen its season of bloom. It needs only the simplest of care, and thrives better when grown on the roots of the wild rose, *Rosa eglanteria*.

As a species, damask roses have traveled widely throughout the entire Mediterranean region. In ancient times they were grown at Marseilles, Paestum, Carthage, and Cyrene. They appear in murals from Pompeii, but the volcanic eruption that destroyed the city seems to have permanently killed off all its damask roses as well, for no wild specimens have been found there since. Many of the Crusaders brought damasks back from Damascus, naming the species for its supposed place of origin. Once the Moslem leader Saladin had driven the Christian invaders out of the city, he had the defiled mosque of Omar purified with five hundred camel-loads of damask-rose water.

Boursault's Rose

[ROSA LHERITIERANEA]

CHARLES LOUIS L'HERITIER DE BRUTELLE was one of Redouté's earliest patrons, and the one who most strongly encouraged Redouté's accuracy in rendering botanical details. Born in Paris in 1746, L'Heritier was a magistrate by profession; but apparently he had sufficient means to pursue his botanical interests on the side. He wrote and financed the publication of several books on botany, including *An English Garland,* an acknowledged masterpiece of its kind. It was ably illustrated by Redouté, who furnished drawings for all his works, and dedicated to English friends of L'Heritier's who had sheltered him when he had fled the French Revolution.

In 1800, L'Heritier was struck down on his own doorstep by an unidentified assassin, and Redouté was moved to commemorate his beloved friend and patron by naming this rose for him. The rose had originally been called Boursault's rose after the horticulturist and botanist Henri Boursault, in whose garden Thory first observed it; so now its common name honors one man and its scientific name another.

Rosa lheritieranea is apparently a hybrid of *R. pendulina,* the alpine brier, and *R. chinensis,* the rose of India. It is a climber that will ascend as high as twenty feet, and it is usually grafted onto the roots of the *rubrifolia,* or red-leaf rose. Boursault's rose is the only hybrid derived from the alpine brier that is equal in quality to the original species.

Ventenat's Rose

[ROSA VENTENATIANA]

THORY RECEIVED SEEDS OF THIS HYBRID in the spring of 1819, and successfully raised it without losing any of its distinguishing characteristics—something not always possible when such plants are bred up from seed. It was a relatively low-growing rose, only two feet high, with fragrant petals of a soft rose color set in four to five rows. It flowered continuously from June to the end of October, and its many small, attractive leaflets crowded around and under the individual blooms, so that the flower appeared to be lying on a bed of leaves. The rose was never common, even in Thory's time, and may have proved difficult to preserve as a variety, for there seems to be no modern record of it.

Since *R. ventenatiana* was intended to memorialize a noted French botanist and horticulturist, it would be sad if it has totally disappeared; but a grafted specimen or two may have survived somewhere. Thory named the variety in honor of Etienne Pierre Ventenat, who was a member of the Institute de France and a librarian at the Bibliothèque de Sainte Geneviève. Ventenat was born in Limoges in 1757, and later went to Paris to practice botany and gardening and to write on related topics. He was the author of *Table of the Vegetable Kingdom,* catalogues of the gardens of Monsieur Cels and those at Malmaison, and numerous scientific articles for learned journals and encyclopedias. He died on April 13, 1808, at the height of his career.

Prairie Rose

[ROSA SETIGERA TOMENTOSA]

THIS ROSE WAS DISCOVERED BY André Michaux in the course of a botanical exploration of America and Canada that he made for the French government between 1785 and 1797. It was not until 1810, however, that the plant became known in Europe. Thory received a living root of this yet unknown rose from a correspondent of his, one Monsieur Sabine, and raised it in his own garden. It showed a tendency to climb—the only native American rose to do so—and offered the chance of improving such climbing hybrids as were then known.

Unluckily, much of the prairie rose's appeal was diminished in Europe because it suffered winter injury in very cold or exposed locations. Moreover, its seeds germinated very slowly, and cuttings were difficult to root; and the flowers, when finally obtained, were almost odorless. Consequently, it never gained much popularity in nineteenth-century gardens, despite its profusion of attractively colored blossoms that appeared from late June through July, extending the flowering season. Few hybrids of the prairie rose occurred in nature because of its tardy period of bloom, combined with a high degree of sterility in its pollen. It was also difficult to breed, for most of the resultant progeny was weak and often incapable of reproducing itself, and so it fell out of cultivation in Europe. But curiously enough, it grew so well in its native eastern and central United States, where huge clumps of it were to be seen in every field and along every roadside, that Michaux named it rose of America. Apparently it preferred to remain untamed, and, like many other wild things, pined in captivity.

Gigantic French Rose

[R O S A   G A L L I C A   F L O R E   G I G A N T E O]

IN ITS DAY, this was one of the largest of all roses (aside from the cabbage roses), producing blossoms more than five inches wide. The old calico prints that once exhibited masses of unbelievably huge flowers on pillow coverings, sofa backs, and window drapes may not have exaggerated floral prowess after all, if they based their designs on such monstrous blooms as these.

This variety was generally grafted, but Thory suspects that in this case, the practice was founded more on custom than necessity. The specimen Thory presented in *Les Roses* had been grown from seed, a more rapid and efficient method of multiplying this rose than grafting. If this rose had been routinely grown from seed, it would have found its way easily and quickly into many more gardens.

Alpine Brier Rose

[ROSA PENDULINA VULGARIS]

THE LIVELY PINK PETALS of the alpine brier are a familiar sight on the slopes of the Alps, the Vosges, the mountains of Auvergne, and the Pyrenées, growing at altitudes of six thousand feet or more. It blooms in those regions from May until the end of July, and in the fall its foliage offers a flaming burst of color.

At the beginning of the nineteenth century it became quite common in cultivation, and the gardeners of that day developed many varieties. Though accustomed to pure mountain air, the rose providentially thrived in the smoke and smog of the dawning industrial age.

While it tends to be somewhat scraggly in the wild, the alpine brier soon fills out under cultivation. The hardy plant actually prefers poor, thin soil, has very few thorns, and manages with little sunshine—all in all, a nearly perfect rose for city gardeners. One thing it will not do, however, is cross with the modern hybrid tea roses, which is a pity, for the hardiness and resistance to disease of the alpine rose would vastly improve the faults still found in the hybrid teas.

White Moss Rose

[ROSA CENTIFOLIA ALBO-MUSCOSA]

THIS IS ONE VARIETY OF ROSE that can be precisely dated and its point of origin firmly placed. The nurseryman Henry Shailer discovered it growing in his gardens at Little Chelsea, London in 1788. It appeared among some other moss roses that he was propagating there, and Shailer knew its worth from the moment he saw it. It took him ten years to develop the rose to the point where he could market it, but his investment of time and labor was soon recovered at the rate of £5 per plant—a very steep price at the end of the eighteenth century. Shailer was lucky to have no rival variety to contend with until 1810, when the superior Bath, or Clifton, white moss appeared.

The original white moss rose was actually a mutation of a mutation, which often happens among centifolia roses. Although it was whiter by far than any moss rose known at that time, it was not a true white, but always had a tinge of blush color. Such mutations are thought to result from incompatibility between the stock and the scion grafted onto it, as was the case here. For proper growth, the rose requires a sheltered situation with much humidity and a minimum of shade.

Steeple Rose

[R O S A C E N T I F O L I A P R O L I F E R A]

THIS UNUSUAL ROSE IS A MODIFICATION of the largest of all the hundred-leaved or cabbage roses, *Rosa centifolia gigantea,* displaying some characteristics of *R. centifolia foliacea,* the leafy cabbage rose, with its own. The long, slender leaves springing out from beneath the flower head are like those of the variety *foliacea* but are much larger and more abundant, hence the term *prolifera.* However, the flower varies to a great extent depending on the conditions it encounters. Soil, sun, atmosphere, and other environmental factors can completely alter its appearance. For that reason André Dupont, who propagated the rose, refused to include it in his nursery catalogues. He kept it true to form by layering, a method of starting new shrubs by burying branch tips still attached to the parent bush.

The name steeple rose came about because frequently a new bud will protrude from the center of a blossom, in an effect reminiscent of a church steeple. Redouté shows this clearly on one flower at the upper left of his picture. The variety is also thought to be the same as the one called king of Holland. Although it is highly valued for the size and perfume of its blossoms, Dupont saved himself much trouble by not marketing it, for it has the disconcerting habit of suddenly producing flowers of ordinary size instead of its usual gigantic ones.

Italian Damask Rose

[ROSA DAMASCENA ITALICA]

THE FLOWERS OF THIS VARIETY are only slightly aromatic, and are valued much more for their color, size, and graceful elegance than for their scent. Precisely when this form of Italian damask came into being is not known. A red variety was extant some years before 1544, and was brought from Italy to France as early as 1580.

Its habit of blooming for a second time, even as late as November, insured the place of *R. damascena italica* in French gardens from the end of the sixteenth century on. Other forms of it either continued to be developed in Italy or occurred naturally there, for André Dupont received a pink variety from Florence in 1795. His gardens at the Luxembourg were not, however, the first to have such specimens, for as many as four varieties, including the pink, had been grown in France at least ten years earlier.

The Italian damask has beautiful flowers that grow up to three inches wide—but *only* when it is grown on its own roots. Those gardeners who make the error of grafting it onto anything else find that the resultant blossoms are much smaller.

Lelieur's Rose

[ROSA DAMASCENA MACROCARPA]

THIS ROSE WAS NAMED FOR Monsieur Lelieur who, as Royal Gardener, had grown it for many years for Louis XVI in the King's Flower Garden at Sèvres. After the Revolution, and during much of Napoleon's career, Lelieur seems to have busied himself in his own garden at Ville-sur-Arce. There he also wrote a book on the cultivation of roses, which was published in Paris in 1811. Because of his close association with this variety, and the wish of those amateur gardeners who had benefited from his book to honor him, this rose came to be named after Lelieur. It was also known as *Lelieur perpetuelle,* from its habit of blooming twice; single Portland; and, after Louis XVIII regained the French throne in 1815, *Rose du roi.*

This rose is extremely thorny, and succeeds best in good soil in a shaded spot in the garden. It is usually propagated through cuttings trimmed off during spring pruning. Its delightfully fragrant flowers are borne in profusion from May to about the end of July. At the height of bloom, its branches are almost entirely covered with flowers. That characteristic, together with its very large fruits, or *macrocarpa,* would seem to indicate a very prolific rose. However, its huge fruits are deceptive since they contain almost no seeds at all; that is why it is grown from cuttings. Luckily, the rose needs only ordinary care in order to thrive.

Marbled Rose

[R O S A   G A L L I C A   F L O R E   M A R M O R E O]

JUST AS WE EXPECT ALL ROSES to have thorns, and find to our surprise that some
don't, so do we tend to think that all roses are sweet-scented. Most are, but
some few perverse ones dispense disagreeable, unroselike odors, while others
have little or no fragrance at all. The marbled rose, while delightful to look at,
is almost entirely lacking in aroma, quite contrary to most other members of its
species, the well-scented French or *gallica* roses. Plants and their workings, it
seems, are no more consistent than human nature.

The large blossoms of the marbled rose are often three inches or more in
diameter, and are almost double. The two or three rows of petals, light rose in
color, are splashed and spotted with a pattern of deeper pink, similar to that in
some types of marble—hence the common and scientific names of this variety.
When grafted onto an understock of eglantine, this rose will thrive better than
on its own roots. Such a situation is frequently encountered among plants, for
some species possess root systems that are superior in one or more respects to
the natural one. If people could trade or combine their genetic heritage as
easily, half our hospitals would be empty.

THE FIRST EDITION OF REDOUTÉ'S *Les Roses* was a very costly book in its time. Measuring twelve by fifteen inches, it sold for about 750 francs, or $1200 in 1979 currency. In addition to the plates already shown, it contained one hundred and one more roses, all of which are reproduced in reduced size on the following pages.

Should the reader be curious as to why the roses shown in this section are not accompanied by common names, there are several valid reasons. First of all, most of them have no common names, being artificially bred varieties. Also, most of them are no longer raised, since many horticultural varieties fall out of fashion every twenty years or so. The names originally assigned by Thory have been retained in this section, although most names dating from this period would have been invalidated several times over by now due to the constant reclassification of roses by taxonomists. But since the majority of these roses died out quickly, it is almost impossible to determine modern names for most of them. Still, while the names of the roses might have changed, Redouté's images of them have not; so no matter what they are called, they rest here for your pleasure.

Rosa gallica agatha parva violacea   Rosa gallica agatha regalis

Rosa centifolia

Rosa geminata

Rosa indica autumnalis

Rosa stylosa

Rosa canina burboniana

Rosa rosenbergiana

Rosa reclinata flore submultiplici

Rosa collina fastigiata

Rosa muscosa anemone-flore

Rosa centifolia flore simplici

Rosa damascena subalba

Rosa eglanteria subrubra

Rosa alba cimbaefolia

Rosa pomponia burgundiaca

Rosa arvensis ovata

Rosa bifera variegata

Rosa orbessanea

Rosa rubiginosa aculeatissima

Rosa indica caryophyllea

Rosa indica subalba

Rosa indica dichotoma

Rosa hispida argentea

Rosa gallica rosea flore simplici

Rosa sempervirens latifolia

Rosa gallica versicolor

Rosa pimpinellifolia alba flore-multiplici

Rosa gallica gueriniana

Rosa rubrifolia

Rosa centifolia carnea

Rosa gallica stapeliae flora

Rosa sempervirens leschenaultiana

Rosa gallica purpurea-violacea magna

Rosa berberifolia

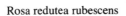

Rosa redutea rubescens

Rosa leucantha

Rosa gallica agatha delphiniana

Rosa bracteata

Rosa alpina debilis

Rosa myriacantha

Rosa montezuma

Rosa damascena celsiana

Rosa cinnamomea maialis

Rosa indica sertulata

Rosa spinulifolia dematratiana

Rosa indica subviolacea

Rosa indica fragrans flore simplici

Rosa villosa pomifera

Rosa pimpinellifolia variegata

Rosa moschata flore semi-pleno

Rosa gallica pontiana

Rosa moschata

Rosa alpina laevis

Rosa indica pumila

Rosa muscosa

Rosa reclinata flore simplici

Rosa sepium rosea

Rosa dumetorum

Rosa banksiae

Rosa indica bengale centifolia

Rosa eglanteria luteola

Rosa indica stelligera

Rosa aciphylla

Rosa rubiginosa flore semi-pleno

Rosa longifolia

Rosa biserrata

Rosa collina monsoniana

Rosa rubiginosa vaillantiana

Rosa gallica latifolia

Rosa alpina flore variegata

Rosa indica

Rosa foetida

Rosa gallica agatha incarnata

Rosa tomentosa

Rosa centifolia crenata

Rosa indica acuminata

Rosa villosa evratina

Rosa pimpinellifolia mariaburgensis

Rosa rubiginosa anemone-flora

Rosa clynophylla

Rosa inermis

Rosa pomponia flore subsimplici

Rosa parviflora

Rosa sempervirens globosa

Rosa rubiginosa cretica

Rosa andegavensis

Rosa indica bengale bichonne

Rosa pimpincllifolia rubra

Rosa indica pumila flore simplici

Rosa sepium myrtifolia

Rosa bifera pumila

Rosa alpina pendulina

Rosa pomponia muscosa

Rosa rubiginosa triflora

Rosa pimpinellifolia pumila

Rosa gallica agatha prolifera

Rosa farinosa

Rosa noisettiana purpurea

Rosa canina nitens

Rosa rubiginosa nemoralis